Popular Concert Favorites

Alto Sax

CD 4126

COMPACT DISC PAGE AND BAND INFORMATION

MMO CD 4126

Music Minus One

Popular Concert Favorites

Alto Saxophone

Band No. Complete Version		Band No. Minus Alto Sax	Page No.
1	Bach: Sarabande	13	4
	Ditterdorf: Tournament of Temperaments:		
2	The Melancholic	14	6
3	The Humble	15	6
4	The Gentle	16	7
5	Schumann: Träumerei	17	5
6	Mendelssohn: Solemn March	18	8
7	Chopin: Prelude	19	12
8	Schubert: Moment Musical	20	9
9	Bizet: Toreador Song	21	10
10	MacDowell: To A Wild Rose	22	12
11	Verdi: Triumphal March (from Aida)	23	13
12	- Tuning Notes, A440 -		

4

Sarabande

J. S. Bach (1685-1750)

Träumerei

Robert Schumann (1810-1856)

Tournament of Temperaments
1. The Melancholic

Ditters von Dittersdorf (1739-1799)

2. The Humble

MMO CD 4126

3. The Gentle

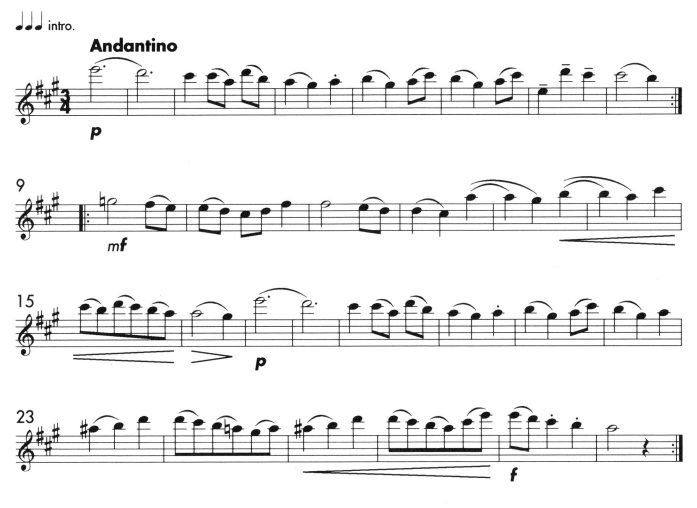

Solemn March

Felix Mendelssohn (1809-1847)

Moment musical

Franz Schubert (1797-1828)

Toreador Song

Georges Bizet (1838-1875)

To a Wild Rose

Edward MacDowell (1860-1908)

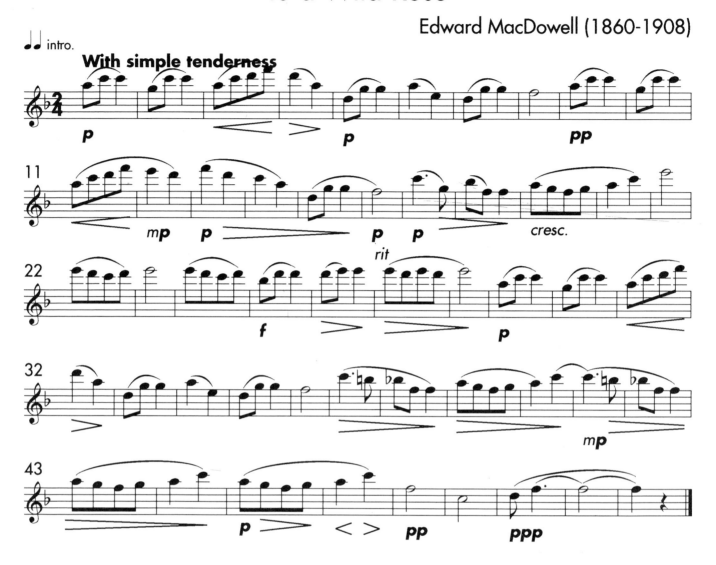

Prelude

Fryderyk Chopin (1810-1849)

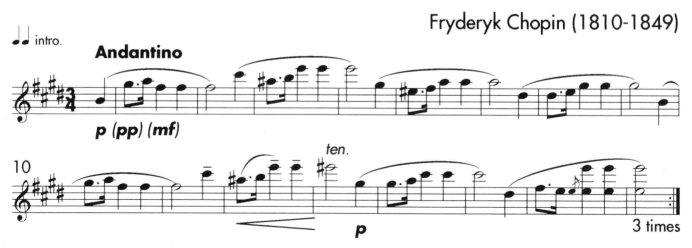

MMO CD 4126

Triumphal March (from *Aida*)

Giuseppe Verdi (1813-1901)

Popular Concert Favorites

Alto Sax

CD 4126

MUSIC MINUS ONE 50 Executive Boulevard • Elmsford New York 10523-1325